global eWorkbook

Contents

Global eWorkbook at a glance

The Global eWorkbook combines the best of both worlds: everything you would find in a printed Workbook for home study and multimedia resources to enhance revision and ongoing learning.

The Global eWorkbooks are mainly intended for self study or home study. They contain a set of resources to support and enhance the material in the Coursebook. The eWorkbook can be used with your computer or you can save some of the material and use it with other devices (for example, mp3 players).

If you prefer to work on paper you can print your work.

When you launch a level of the Global eWorkbooks you will see the following options:

Where to start?

You can start by going to help  or by reading this booklet.

If you want to have a clear overview of the whole content you should select the Contents Map icon.

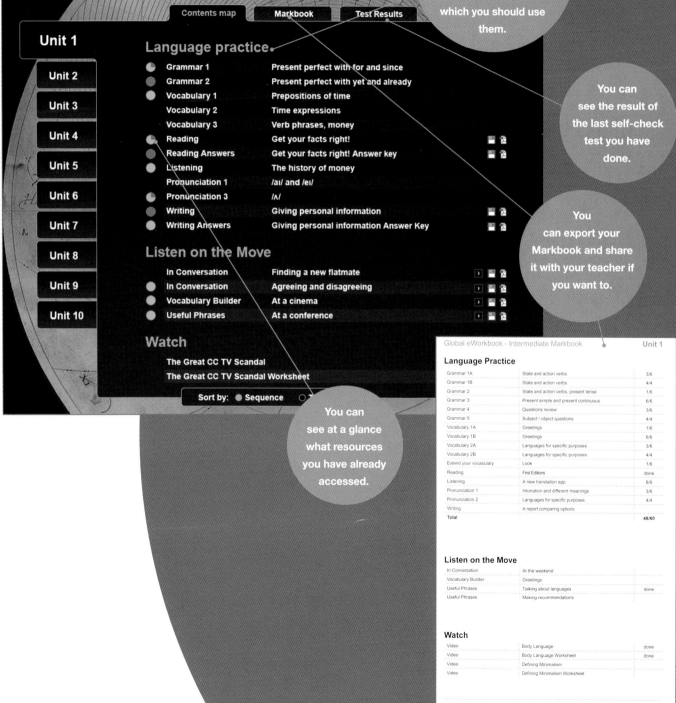

You can see all the resources linked to each of the units, and you can view them either by type or by the recommended order in which you should use them.

You can see the result of the last self-check test you have done.

You can export your Markbook and share it with your teacher if you want to.

You can see at a glance what resources you have already accessed.

Language Practice

LANGUAGE PRACTICE

The Language Practice section includes activities that provide consolidation of the language presented in the Coursebook. It includes practice of all language skills: grammar, vocabulary, pronunciation, reading, listening and writing.

global
INTERMEDIATE — eWorkbook

LANGUAGE PRACTICE

BY UNIT

| Unit 1 | Unit 2 | Unit 3 | Unit 4 | Unit 5 |
| Unit 6 | Unit 7 | Unit 8 | Unit 9 | Unit 10 |

BY SKILL

Functional language	Grammar	Listening
Pronunciation	Reading	Vocabulary
Writing		

One of the advantages of an eWorkbook is that you can do the exercises as many times as you want. Most of the exercises are interactive. Reading and Writing activities are printable PDFs.

You can navigate the material by unit or by language skill. If you choose to work by unit, you will be taken to a list of all the activities related to that particular unit.

If you choose to work by skill, you will be taken to a list of all the different activities related to that particular skill.

global
INTERMEDIATE — eWorkbook

LANGUAGE PRACTICE

UNIT 1

Grammar 1	Present perfect with for and since
Grammar 2	Present perfect with yet and already
Vocabulary 1	Prepositions of time
Vocabulary 2	Time expressions
Vocabulary 3	Verb phrases, money
Vocabulary	borrow and lend
Reading	Time to think
Listening	The history of money
Pronunciation 1	/aɪ/ and /eɪ/
Pronunciation 2	Sentence stress
Pronunciation 3	/ʌ/
Writing	Giving your opinion

When you choose an activity practising grammar, vocabulary, listening or pronunciation you will be taken to a screen like this one.

| Unit 1 | Vocabulary 2 | Languages for specific purposes |

Complete the sentences with the correct type of language.

1. I work for a large Chinese company and we have customers all over the world, so I need b [____] English for my work.

2. I'm an architect and I've been working in Dubai. Sometimes it was difficult because the builders didn't know enough t [____] English, and I don't speak Arabic!

3. I'm a translator for an international law firm based in Spain, so I have a good knowledge of l [____] English and Spanish.

4. I'm from Russia, and I work as a biologist. Sometimes I find it hard to have a normal conversation in E[____] but my s [____] English is very good!

5. All doctors who volunteer to work with us in Togo have to speak French, but most need to do a cou[____] m [____] French before they start.

6. I'm from Sri Lanka so I speak good English, but because I'm a pilot I had to study a [____] E[____] as part of my training.

Whichever way you work you will always be able to access the following resources: Dictionary, Grammar Help, Word Lists and Writing Tips.

| Check answers | Show answers | Try again | | ≪ | Menu | ≫ |

Unit 1   **Vocabulary 1A**   **Greetings**

Write a word in each gap to complete the greetings. Contractions count as one word.

1 A: G _____ m _____ .
   B: Ah, h _____ , Mr Emery. We weren't expecting you until this afternoon.
   A: I know, but I managed to get an earlier flight.

2 A: E _____ !
   B: Oh, h _____ Stig. I haven't seen you for ages. H _____ a _____ t _____ ?
   A: Good. What about you?

3 A: H _____
   B: H _____ t _____ , Polly. H _____ i _____ g _____ ?
   A: Not too bad, thanks. Listen, have you got a moment?

4 A: G _____ e _____ . Can I help you?
   B: Yes, I'm looking for the conference room. Could you tell me where it is?

_____rs   Try again   ✖ ≪ Menu ≫

print_and_work_Unit1.pdf

Create ▾   Combine ▾   Collaborate ▾   Secure ▾   Sign ▾   Forms ▾   Multimedia ▾   Comment ▾

1 / 2   100% ▾   Find

Language & Culture

Reading
First Editions

1 Write the years, numbers and prices using numbers, letters and symbols.

1 first
2 one thousand five hundred
3 one thousand five hundred and sixty pounds
4 the year two thousand and eight
5 thirty thousand pounds
6 one hundred million

2 Look at the magazine article and find the numbers to check your answers.

3 Read the article and use the numbers in exercise 1 to complete the sentences.

1 Bonhams auctioned a copy of *The Hobbit* in _____ .
2 Experts thought the book would sell for _____ .
3 Only _____ copies of the first edition were printed.
4 Over the years the book has sold more than _____ copies.
5 At the auction the first foreign language edition of the book sold for _____ .
6 Look for the number 1 on the copyright page to see if your book is a _____ edition.

4 Answer the questions. Then read the article again to check your answers.

1 Does a printing mistake make a first edition more or less valuable?
2 Why was the auctioned copy of *The Hobbit* valuable?
3 Who was Elaine Griffiths?
4 Which language was the book first translated into?
5 How many translations exist today?

print_and_work_Unit1.pdf

Create ▾   Combine ▾   Collaborate ▾   Secure ▾   Sign ▾   Forms ▾   Multimedia ▾   Comment ▾

2 / 2   100% ▾   Find

Language & Culture

Writing
A report comparing options
Reading

1 What type of things do you have to write as part of your work or studies? Add to the list below.
Essays about subjects related to my degree
Emails to organise meetings

2 Read the email. Is this type of writing on your list? What is its purpose? What do you think the relationship between Jaya and Morwena is?

Dear Morwena,

As requested, I've looked into the options available for providing Spanish tuition to our employees. I've outlined what I consider to be the pros and cons of each one below.

The first option is evening classes, consisting of two 90-minute classes a week over a nine-month period. The advantage of evening classes is that because they take place after work, people are less likely to miss them because of meetings, *etc.* The downside

3 Complete the table with information from the email.

Providing Spanish tuition		
Option	Advantages	Disadvantages

Writing skills: presenting advantages and disadvantages

4 What other words and phrases in the email report mean the same as advantage(s) or disadvantages(s)? Write them in the spaces below.

advantage(s): _____ , _____ ,

disadvantage(s): _____ ,

Print and Work

PRINT AND WORK

This section offers a pen-and-paper version of the activities in the Language Practice section, plus downloadable audio tracks when needed. It is designed to suit a different learning style. If you prefer to work away from the computer, this gives you exactly the same as what you would expect in a printed workbook with the added advantage that you only print the pages that you need.

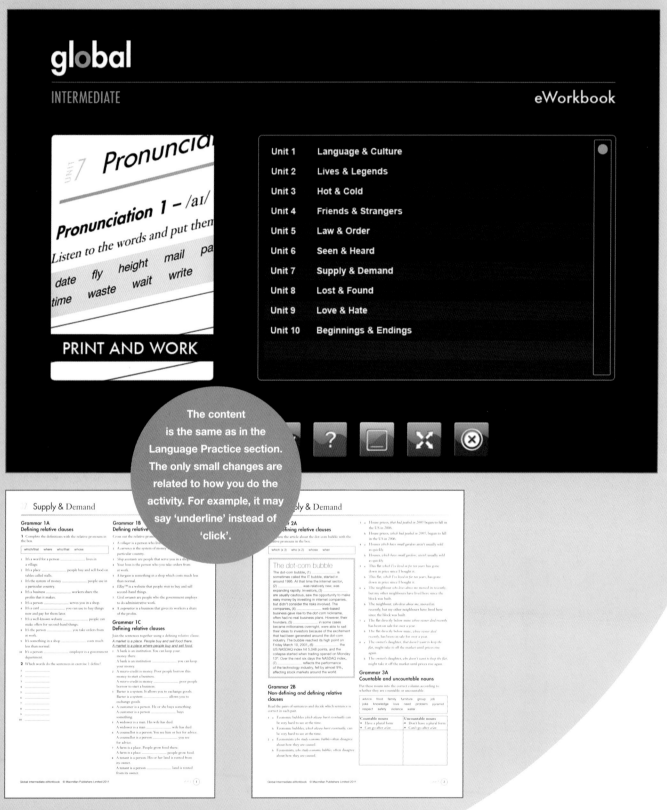

There is an answer key provided as a PDF.

If audio files are needed to complete an activity, you will have the option of playing them or downloading them.

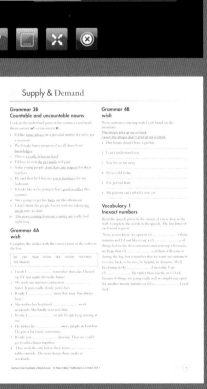

Listen

LISTEN

This section offers access to all the Listening material in the eWorkbook.
It includes the following:

- Access to the listening activities in the Language Practice section
- Audio material designed to be used 'on the move'

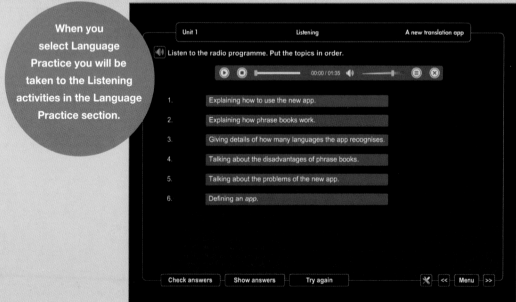

When you select Language Practice you will be taken to the Listening activities in the Language Practice section.

Listen on the Move includes audio material not linked to specific activities, i.e. different from the listening material in the Language Practice section. There are three types of audio material.

Useful Phrases features mini-dialogues that contain the 'Useful phrases' in the Coursebook (e.g. 'agreeing and disagreeing').

In Conversation contains situational dialogues (e.g. at a restaurant, taking a taxi). The situations relate to the situations in the 'Function Globally' pages in the Coursebook.

Vocabulary Builder contains lists of vocabulary items introduced in the Coursebook which are organised by topic.

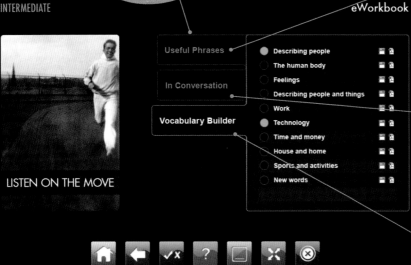

You can play this material by clicking on play or you can download the files and copy them onto an mp3 player or other devices.

You can also print or download a PDF with the audioscript for all this material.

As its name indicates, this is ideal for learning on the move.

Watch

When you select Watch in the main menu you are taken to a screen where all the video clips in the eWorkbook are listed.

You can either watch the videos on your computer or download the files. When you watch the videos on your computer you can select to watch them with or without subtitles.

When you click on 'download' you can copy the files to a selected location. You can download the files in a number of formats, for example for iPod, iTouch, iPhone or other common mobile phones.

You can also download the scripts as a PDF.

Body language

Length: 1.32

Language
Using gestures to communicate
Adjectives
Parts of the head and body

Possible uses
You can watch the video on your computer or download it onto a portable device. You can choose to watch it with or without subtitles. Don't try to understand every word when you watch. Use the pause and cursor controls to watch parts of the video again. There are exercises on this activity sheet to complete before you watch, while you're watching, and after you watch.

Before you watch
1 Use your hands to communicate these messages without speaking.
1 Hi!
2 OK.
3 Stop!
4 Come here!
5 Be quiet.
6 I'm thinking.

While you watch
2 Watch the first part of the video to check your answers to exercise 1.

3 Watch the rest of the video without subtitles and complete the phrases with the words in the box.

bored defensive depressed don't know funny interested

I (1) _____
I'm confused.
I'm (2) _____
I'm exhausted.
I'm (3) _____
I'm relaxed.
I'm thinking about something else.
I'm (4) _____
I'm not interested.
I'm not here.
You are so (5) _____
I'm shocked.
I'm (6) _____

4 Watch the final part of the video. What are the final three things he 'says'?
1
2
3

5 Watch the complete video with subtitles to check your answers to exercises 3 and 4.

After you watch
6 Read the descriptions and match them with some of the phrases in exercise 3.
1 He closes his eyes.
2 He moves his shoulders up and down.
3 He puts his arms behind his head.
4 He nods his head without showing interest.
5 He wipes the sweat from his brow.
6 He opens his mouth and quickly moves his hand to cover it.

There are accompanying worksheets, available as printable PDFs, one per unit. These include comprehension questions and language work and can be used when you watch the video material on your computer or on the move.

There are two video clips per unit. It is authentic material suitable for intermediate learners.

The video clips follow a similar style to the user-generated content available on popular video websites.

On the Move

ON THE MOVE

This section includes content also accessible through the Listen and Watch sections offered in one place for ease of access.

When you select this option you are taken to a screen that offers you the option of downloading audio material or video material.

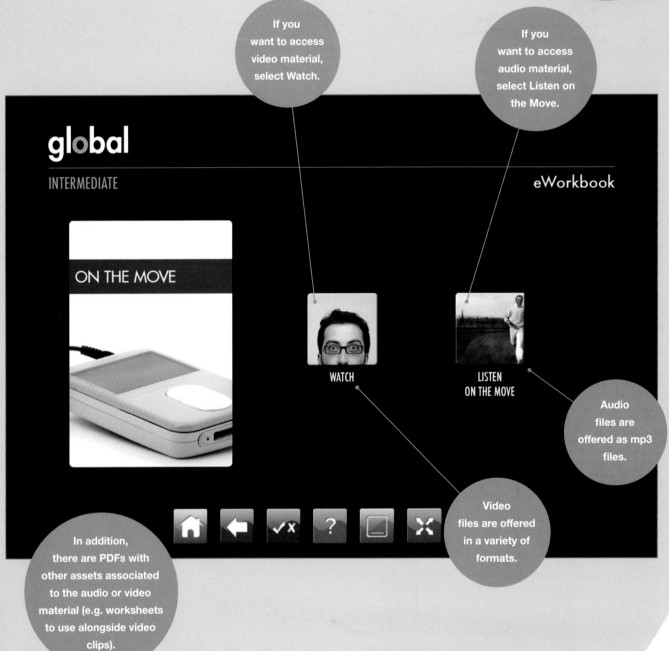

If you want to access video material, select Watch.

If you want to access audio material, select Listen on the Move.

Audio files are offered as mp3 files.

Video files are offered in a variety of formats.

In addition, there are PDFs with other assets associated to the audio or video material (e.g. worksheets to use alongside video clips).

Reference Tools

DICTIONARY

WORD LISTS

GRAMMAR HELP

WRITING TIPS

The Global eWorkbook contains powerful Reference Tools to help you with your work.

These tools can be accessed directly from the main menu on the home page or when you are doing an activity.

The Dictionary Tool is a link to the Macmillan English Dictionary Online (you need to be online to access this feature).

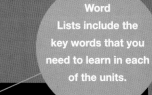

Word Lists include the key words that you need to learn in each of the units.

If you select Grammar Help, you can choose from a list of grammar items and get all the relevant information.

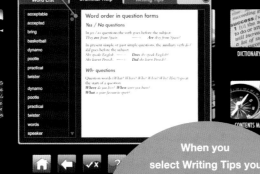

When you select Writing Tips you are given a list of topics. Each of them includes a brief explanation on a particular aspect of writing, such as the use of capital letters, spelling, punctuation, paragraphing, etc., followed by a series of multiple-choice questions to ensure that the main points have been understood.

Tests and Portfolio

TESTS   PORTFOLIO

You can test yourself at any point using the Global eWorkbook. You can set yourself tests either by a set time or a set number of questions from any unit.

When you finish the test you will be given a score. Your last three scores will be recorded.

When you select Portfolio in the main menu you are taken to a screen offering information about the Common European Framework, User needs, Language passport and Self-assessment Checklists.